Previous page: The publishing house of Artaria on the Kohlmarkt in Vienna. Several of Beethoven's compositions were published by the cousins, Francesco and Carlo Artaria.

Below: The Theater an der Wien, Vienna, where several of Beethoven's compositions were heard for the first time.

BEETHOVEN
and His World

Alan Kendall

SILVER BURDETT

Contents

Editorial

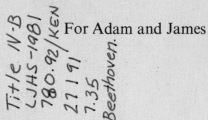

Author
Alan Kendall

Editor
Jane Olliver

Illustrators
Roger Payne
Roger Phillips

For Adam and James

Title IV-B
LJHS-1981
780.92/KEN
27191
7.35
1. Beethoven.

A KINGFISHER BOOK

Published in the United States by
Silver Burdett Company, Morristown, New
Jersey.

1980 Printing

ISBN 0-382-06375-9

Designed and produced by Grisewood & Dempsey Limited,
Grosvenor House, 141-143 Drury Lane, London WC2.

The Romantic Era

The Romantic Era produced a new wave of literature, paintings and music in the late 18th century. Romantic styles, which stressed imagination and freedom, replaced classical styles. Romanticism was evident in the works of such writers as Goethe and Wordsworth, such artists as Delacroix and Turner and such composers as Wagner, Schubert and Beethoven.

In Beethoven we see much of what makes up the romantic character. He stands for the freedom and independence of the artist. He also shows his need to follow his own artistic ideas. By the time he died, Beethoven had made a new role for the composer in society. However, he did not deliberately set out to do this. What he did do was to follow his beliefs, both in his life and his work.

Beethoven's life was an important milestone in man's increasing understanding of his own nature and personality. He was, above all, an individual. His life and work cannot be separated from the man himself. It is for this reason that we come to look upon Beethoven as the standard-bearer of the Romantic Era.

The Romantic movement inspired many great musicians. Here Liszt plays the piano with a volume of Beethoven's sonatas in front of him. On the right is Ernst, the violinist, and on the left is Kriehuber. Standing are Berlioz and Czerny.

Beethoven's World

Beethoven's world was a compact one. Almost all of the important events at the time – apart from American affairs – were happening in Western Europe. From his home in Vienna, Beethoven could deal with publishers in Edinburgh as easily as with patrons in St Petersburg.

It was the time of the Napoleonic Wars and the French Revolution. It was also the time of other great musicians such as Mozart and Haydn, such artists as Goya and Constable and such writers as Goethe and Schiller.

NORWAY

Bergen

Oslo

Stockholm

SCOTLAND
Burns 1759–96
(Poet)
Edinburgh
Scott 1771–1832
(Novelist and poet)

Wordsworth 1770–1850 (Poet)

SWEDEN
Linnaeus 1707–78
(Botanist)

IRELAND

DENMARK
Copenhagen

Dublin

NORTH SEA

H C Andersen 1805–75
(Writer)

Goldsmith 1728–74
(Writer)

WALES ENGLAND

Weber 1786–1826
(Composer)

Hamburg

LONDON
Turner 1775–1851
(Painter)

Blake 1757–1827
(Artist and poet)

Byron 1788–1824
(Poet)

Constable 1776–1837 (Painter)

Darwin 1809–82
(Naturalist)
London

Plymouth
Reynolds
1723–92
(Painter)

Dickens 1812–70
(Novelist)

NETHERLANDS
Amsterdam Bremen

Kierkegaard 1813–55
(Philosopher)

Mendelssohn 1809–4
(Composer)

Berlin

Schiller 1759–1805
(Poet and dramatist)

Lille

Brussels Cologne Weimar

Leipzig

Wagner 1813–83
(Composer)

Bonn

Franck 1822–90
(Composer)

Rouen

Lamarck 1744–1829
(Naturalist)

Frankfurt

Goethe 1749–1832
(Writer)

Prague

HOLY

Schuma
1810–5
(Compo

Paris

Voltaire 1694–1778
(Philosopher and writer)

Strasbourg

ROMAN

Munich EMPIRE

Vien

Loire

Balzac
1799–1850
(Novelist)

Dijon

Zurich

Salzburg

Mozart 1756–91
(Composer)

FRANCE

Geneva

ALPS

Haydn 1732–18
(Composer)

Bordeaux

Lyons

Ampère
1775–1836
(Scientist)

Rousseau
1712–78
Philosopher
and writer

Verona

Venice

Milan

Po

Donizetti 1797–1848
(Composer)

Garonne

Rhône

Berlioz 1803–69
(Composer)

Genoa

Bologna

Verdi 1813–1901
(Opera composer)

Ebro

Marseilles

Garibaldi 1807–82
(Italian patriot)

Toulon

Douro

PYRENEES

Tiber

PORTUGAL

Tagus

SPAIN

Zaragoza

Madrid

Goya 1746–1828
(Painter)

Barcelona

**Napoleon
Bonaparte**
1769–1821
(Emperor of
the French)

Rome

ITALY

Lisbon

Guadiana

Naples

Guadalquivir

Seville

MEDITERRANEAN SEA

Palermo

Bellini 1801–35
(Opera composer)

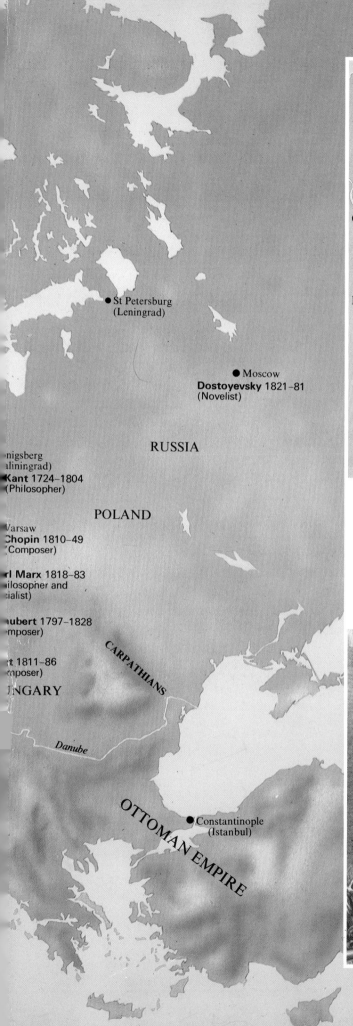

St Petersburg
(Leningrad)

Moscow
Dostoyevsky 1821–81
(Novelist)

RUSSIA

nigsberg
aliningrad)
Kant 1724–1804
(Philosopher)

POLAND

Warsaw
Chopin 1810–49
(Composer)

rl Marx 1818–83
ilosopher and
cialist)

ubert 1797–1828
mposer)

rt 1811–86
mposer)

NGARY

CARPATHIANS

Danube

OTTOMAN EMPIRE

Constantinople
(Istanbul)

Weser
Elbe
Oder

Berlin

Cologne
Bonn
Kassel
Leipzig
Weimar
Dresden

Koblenz
Frankfurt

Mainz
Prague

Mannheim
Heidelberg
Nuremberg

Rhine
Danube

Stuttgart

Augsburg
Munich
Linz
VIENNA
Mödling
Baden
Salzburg

THE ALPS

Above: Beethoven's immediate world centered on Vienna. It stretched northwest to Bonn and the Rhine Valley and north to Prague, Dresden, Leipzig and Berlin.

Below: The storming of the Bastille, a fortress-prison in Paris, in 1789. Beethoven's times were those of both the French and the American revolutions.

Early Years in Bonn

Ludwig van Beethoven was born in Bonn, now the capital of West Germany, in 1770. His family originally came from Malines in Belgium. Beethoven's father was a musician at the court of the Elector of Cologne, as was his grandfather. Although the official capital of the state over which the Elector ruled was the city of Cologne, his residence was in Bonn. This is how the Beethoven family came to live there. Young Ludwig always thought of Bonn with affection. Even when he went to live in Vienna, he continued to dream of the day that he would return.

Beethoven's grandfather – also called Ludwig – eventually became Kapellmeister (Master of Music) at the Electoral court. Beethoven always had fond memories of his grandfather, despite the fact that he was only three years old when he died. Of Beethoven's father, Johann, the memory was not so happy. Johann was not such a good musician as his father, and certainly less talented than his son. He also drank heavily, which caused great hardship for the family, especially his wife. Beethoven was very devoted to his mother, and her death, when he was 17, had a deep effect on him. However, at least Johann recognized his son's talent, and his efforts helped Beethoven to develop it to the full.

Right: The house in the Bonngasse in Bonn where Beethoven was born. The Beethoven family moved from this house in 1774, when Ludwig was just four years old. Today the building houses an archive and museum to the composer's memory.

Below: In the late 18th century Bonn was a delightful small town on the banks of the River Rhine. The palace of the Electors, which looked so impressive from the river, was seriously damaged by fire in 1777 and rebuilt.

R Phillips '79

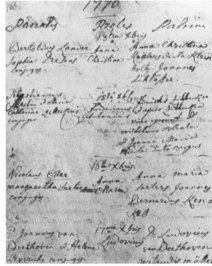

*Above: Beethoven's grandfather
Ludwig (1712–1773), left, and
father Johann (1740–1792),
center. Beethovén's mother Maria
Magdalena, right, died in 1787.*

*Far left: Beethoven was baptised
on the 17th of December 1770, as
we can see from the bottom entry
in the register of St Remigius's
Church. He was probably born on
the 15th or 16th of that month.*

*Left: The room in which
Beethoven was born.*

The Young Musician

Beethoven's first lessons for piano and violin – and possibly viola – were from his father. Although he was not an infant prodigy, it soon became obvious that the young Ludwig had possibilities. Johann arranged a public concert in Bonn in 1778, when he presented Beethoven as a year younger than he really was. As a result of that early start, Johann realized that he must look elsewhere for teachers for his son. He sought help from his colleagues on the musical staff at court, and in particular Christian Gottlob Neefe, the organist. Neefe's influence was vital to the developing Ludwig and through him he gained a firm musical grounding. Beethoven was also encouraged to look beyond the rather limited musical world of Bonn. He was attracted to what was happening in Vienna, capital of the Austrian Empire. So early in 1787 Beethoven set out for Vienna but he had to return to Bonn later in that year when he heard that his mother was dying.

Above: Christian Gottlob Neefe (1748–98) who was Beethoven's first important teacher and musical influence.

Below left: The organ which Beethoven played at the age of nine in the Minorite Monastery in Bonn.

Below: The poster for Beethoven's first public appearance. He was seven at the time although his father put his age at six.

Above: The arrival of the Elector Maximilian Franz by boat in Bonn in 1780 as portrayed by the artist F J Roussaux.

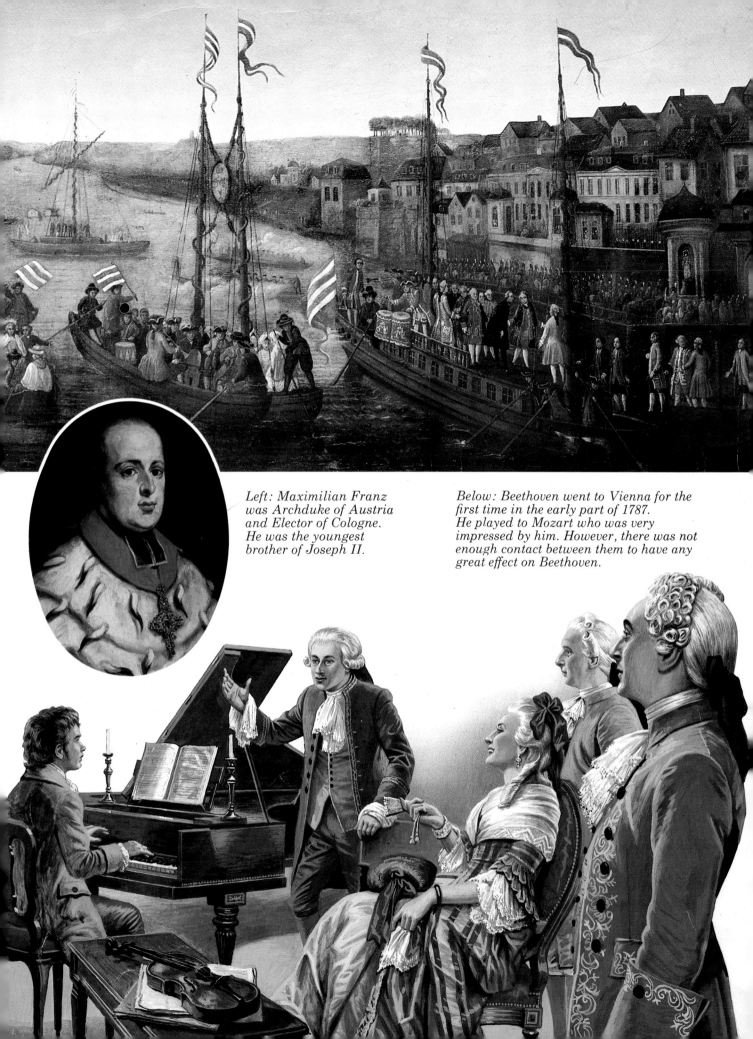

Left: Maximilian Franz
was Archduke of Austria
and Elector of Cologne.
He was the youngest
brother of Joseph II.

Below: Beethoven went to Vienna for the
first time in the early part of 1787.
He played to Mozart who was very
impressed by him. However, there was not
enough contact between them to have any
great effect on Beethoven.

Court Life

Music played a very important part in life at court, especially for religious services, but also for state occasions and court entertainments. When Beethoven returned to Bonn from Vienna he was appointed assistant organist and was also a viola player in the court orchestra. In the winter season of 1788 the Elector organized a theater company, and Beethoven was engaged to play in that orchestra. In all he took part in five such seasons. As well as helping the family with money, Beethoven's work at court gained him valuable experience of orchestral practice and composition. In 1790 he met Haydn who was on his way to England. Haydn returned to Bonn from England in 1792 and it was probably then decided that Beethoven would go to Vienna to study with him.

By now Beethoven had become friendly with two families who gave him encouragement and support. They were the von Breunings and the von Waldsteins. It was Count Ferdinand von Waldstein, a close friend of the Elector, who encouraged Beethoven to write his *Ritterballet*, and the composer dedicated one of his greatest piano sonatas to the count.

Below: The palace of the Electors at Bonn before it was rebuilt after the fire of 1777. Three generations of Beethovens were employed as court musicians.

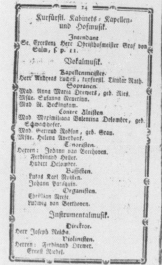
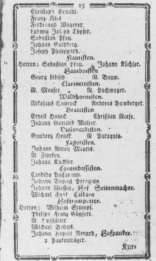

Above: A list of the court musicians on the staff at Bonn in 1788. This was after Beethoven's return from his first visit to Vienna, when a theater company was formed by the Elector.

Left: A silhouette portrait of the young Beethoven in court dress.

Below: The gala dress of the court musicians was very colorful. It consisted of a sea-green coat, green breeches worn with white or black silk stockings, and a flowered silk waistcoat.

Clarinet

Oboe

Cello

Viola

Classical guitar

Some musical instruments used in Beethoven's time (not to scale).

Organ

Harpsichord

Beethoven's Vienna

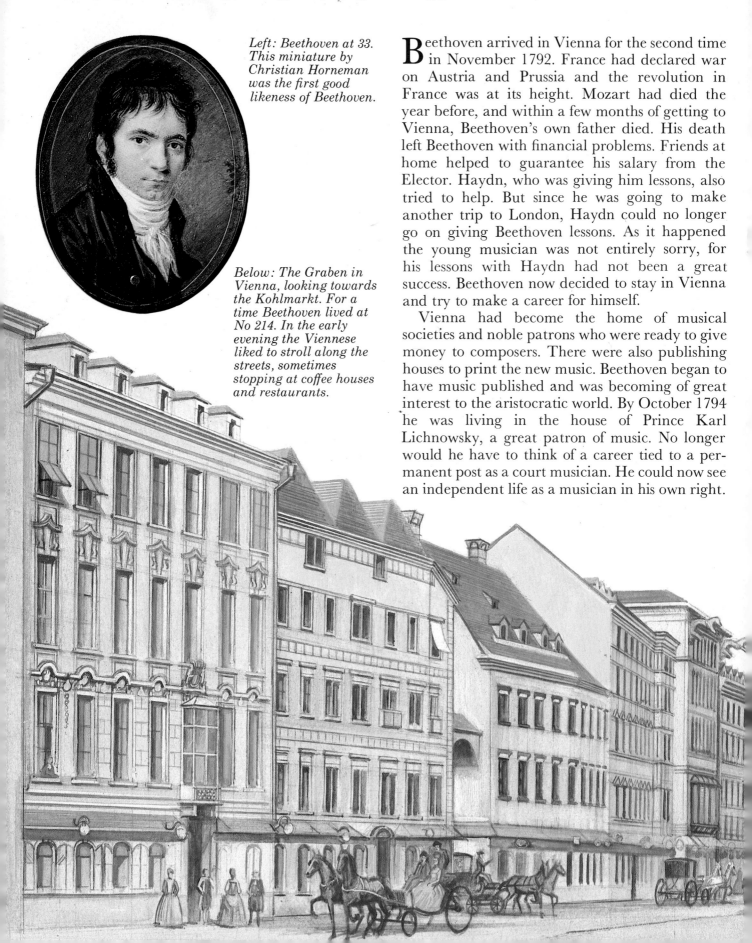

Left: Beethoven at 33. This miniature by Christian Horneman was the first good likeness of Beethoven.

Below: The Graben in Vienna, looking towards the Kohlmarkt. For a time Beethoven lived at No 214. In the early evening the Viennese liked to stroll along the streets, sometimes stopping at coffee houses and restaurants.

Beethoven arrived in Vienna for the second time in November 1792. France had declared war on Austria and Prussia and the revolution in France was at its height. Mozart had died the year before, and within a few months of getting to Vienna, Beethoven's own father died. His death left Beethoven with financial problems. Friends at home helped to guarantee his salary from the Elector. Haydn, who was giving him lessons, also tried to help. But since he was going to make another trip to London, Haydn could no longer go on giving Beethoven lessons. As it happened the young musician was not entirely sorry, for his lessons with Haydn had not been a great success. Beethoven now decided to stay in Vienna and try to make a career for himself.

Vienna had become the home of musical societies and noble patrons who were ready to give money to composers. There were also publishing houses to print the new music. Beethoven began to have music published and was becoming of great interest to the aristocratic world. By October 1794 he was living in the house of Prince Karl Lichnowsky, a great patron of music. No longer would he have to think of a career tied to a permanent post as a court musician. He could now see an independent life as a musician in his own right.

Vienna, Capital of an Empire

Vienna, situated on the River Danube, was the capital of the Austrian Empire under the Hapsburgs. The Hapsburg family ruled in central Europe from the 1200s until after World War I. During Beethoven's time the emperor was also the Holy Roman Emperor. He was the elected head of a group of several states that today roughly make up Germany and Austria.

In the 1700s and 1800s Vienna became the center of the social, economic and artistic life of the greater part of Europe. At the time of Beethoven's arrival, the city was at the height of its magnificence. It had an excellent university and public library as well as many fine theaters. People would gather in coffee houses to talk about politics and the arts.

All the arts were important in Vienna, but music, especially Italian music, took first place. Music was enjoyed by all. It was played in homes and in the street as well as in concert halls and in the Imperial Court itself.

Above: Beethoven congratulates Haydn (center foreground) after a performance of Haydn's Creation *in the University hall in Vienna, 1808.*

Haydn (1732–1809), far left, was the father figure of Viennese music. He and Mozart (1756–1791), left, led the great Viennese classical school.

The Countryside

Above: Views of Teplitz (Teplice, now in Czechoslovakia), the spa Beethoven first visited in the summer of 1811. It was here that he met Amalie von Sebald and Goethe.

Below: The spa of Heiligenstadt, near Vienna. The peace and quiet, within easy reach of the capital, made it a favorite retreat for Beethoven in summer.

During the summer months Beethoven liked to spend as much time as possible away from the bustle of Vienna, for it seemed a vast place after Bonn. Early in his second visit to Vienna he went with Haydn to the Esterházy Palace at Eisenstadt. A similar aristocratic home visited by Beethoven was the Lichnowsky castle near Gratz in Czechoslovakia. Beethoven often worried about the company he might find himself in at such grand places. It was often very pleasant but there were some occasions when he wished he had not gone. But Beethoven enjoyed his stays in the villages around Vienna. Here he was close enough to return for business quickly if need be. At the same time he could enjoy the peace and the simple life of the countryside. Heiligenstadt was one of his favorites. It was there that he wrote both the Fifth and Sixth Symphonies, but later Hetzendorf, Baden, Mödling, Nussdorf and Döbling all attracted him.

Above: Goethe (1749–1832) was a German novelist, poet and playwright. He is one of the most important figures in European literature. Beethoven greatly admired Goethe. They met at the spa of Teplitz in 1812 but no lasting friendship was formed.

Above: In the peaceful surroundings of Mödling Beethoven composed most of the Missa Solemnis *and the Ninth Symphony.*

Beethoven's Travels

Beethoven made several visits to the countryside around Vienna. He also traveled further afield, especially in his early days in the capital. Early in 1796, for example, he went on a concert tour to Prague with Prince Lichnowsky. The Prince had been there before with Mozart. After a swift return to Vienna, Beethoven set out for Leipzig, Dresden and Berlin, where he played to the King of Prussia. One of his great hopes was to visit London, but this was never fulfilled. He also considered going to Kassel as Kapellmeister to Napoleon's brother Jérôme, then King of Westphalia. Happily for the Viennese this never happened. In fact, it was as a result of this threat that a contract was drawn up by some of the composer's aristocratic friends. This contract guaranteed him a regular income. In the summer of 1811 Beethoven went to the spa at Teplitz in Czechoslovakia where he made a new circle of friends. On his return there the next year he was introduced to Goethe. Although the meeting went quite well, the two men did not form a friendship, nor did they feel inspired to work together on a project.

Revolution and Freedom

Beethoven had sympathised with republican ideas since his time at Bonn University. He took great interest in the French Revolution and in the birth of the French Republic. He admired its leader, Napoleon, and intended dedicating his Third or *Eroica* Symphony to him. It would indeed have been a fitting tribute, for the *Eroica* was a landmark in the development of the symphony and twice as long as anything similar by Mozart or Haydn. However, when Beethoven was told that Napoleon had crowned himself emperor, the composer was disgusted and changed his dedication. Later, Beethoven seemed to hate anything French, and certainly he had some unfortunate experiences. The invasion of Vienna by Napoleon's army in 1805, for example, happened to occur at the same time as the first performance of Beethoven's opera *Fidelio*. In the circumstances the Viennese had deserted the opera houses, and such audiences as there were tended to be French. It was unlikely, then, that the opera would have been a success. Beethoven revised it in 1806, and again for the 1814 performances, when it finally gained its deserved success. The basic themes, of devoted married love and freedom in the face of tyranny, were ones close to Beethoven's heart. They had particular emphasis and sadness because Beethoven never married and also because of the events that shook Europe during the Napoleonic era.

Above: Beethoven scratched "Bonaparte" off the title page of the score of his Third or Eroica Symphony when he heard that Napoleon had crowned himself emperor.

Left: A 19th-century set design for the dungeon scene of Act II of Fidelio.

Right (inset): Napoleon Bonaparte (1769–1821).

Right: Vienna fell to Napoleon in 1805 and 1809. This picture shows the bombardment of the city by the French troops in 1809.

The Great Master

As 1808 drew to its close Beethoven presented several major works, all in the course of one evening. On the 22nd of December he gave a concert at the Theater an der Wien which included the Fifth Symphony, the Choral Fantasia, the Piano Concerto in G (Op. 58) and various movements of the Mass for Princess Esterházy (Op. 86). Even after this success Beethoven felt that he had not won the place he deserved in the hearts of the Viennese. As a result, he seriously thought of leaving the city at the beginning of 1809. But three aristocratic patrons drew up a contract in March of that year and persuaded him to stay. Although Beethoven was never really rich, he was never short of money.

In May of that year Napoleon invaded Vienna, forcing Beethoven to hide in a cellar during the bombardment. In the same month Haydn died. There was now no one to challenge Beethoven's right to be the musical king of Vienna. He was at

Above: Franz Lein's bronze bust of Beethoven was based on a mask he took of the composer in 1812. It is therefore the best likeness we have of Beethoven.

Above: The piano given to Beethoven by Thomas Broadwood in 1818.

that very moment writing the Fifth Piano Concerto – known as the *Emperor* – a title he would hardly have approved of, with Napoleon occupying the Schönbrunn Palace. Then, at the end of 1813, the Seventh Symphony was performed for the first time. Meanwhile, Beethoven had spent two summers at Teplitz and had written the letter to the ''Immortal Beloved''. The première of the Seventh Symphony, together with *Wellington's Victory* or *The Battle of Vittoria*, gave Beethoven the public recognition he wanted. He also made a lot of money that he was able to invest in bank shares. He refused to touch these shares for he was determined to leave them to his nephew Karl.

The year 1814 saw repeated success for both *Wellington's Victory* and the Seventh Symphony, as well as for *Fidelio*. Unfortunately, domestic problems were soon to spoil this success. Beethoven's brother Casper Anton Carl died in 1815, and the composer became guardian of his son Karl. Beethoven's increasing deafness was another problem. It made it impossible for him to conduct his works or even perform any more.

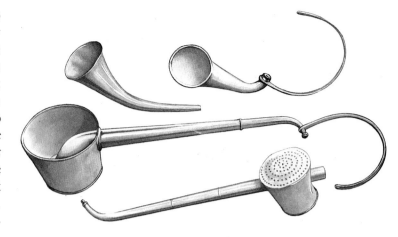

Above: Beethoven began to suffer from deafness in about 1796, but he told no one until about five years later. In the summer of 1802 his doctor sent him to the country spa of Heiligenstadt (see page 18) to rest. It was here that he wrote a document called the Heiligenstadt Testament. Addressed to his brothers, the document describes the unhappiness and worry that his increasing deafness was causing him. Shown here are some of the ear trumpets that he used to try and improve his hearing. Today a simple operation or a hearing aid would probably have been able to cure Beethoven's deafness.

Immortal Beloved

The three-part letter written to an unnamed woman known to history as the ''Immortal Beloved'' (though ''Eternally Beloved'' is more accurate), was written by Beethoven on the 6th and 7th of July, 1812. The letter expresses Beethoven's love for a woman who shared his feelings but could not marry him. It was found among his belongings after his death, so it is unlikely that it was ever sent. Naturally many people have tried to find out the name of the woman to whom the letter was written. Therese von Brunsvik took piano lessons from Beethoven, and she remained a close friend. But it is thought that he was more attracted to her sister Josephine. He also wanted to marry Therese von Malfatti, but her family was against the idea. Amalie von Sebald was one of the group of friends Beethoven made in Teplitz in 1811. His affection for her never seems to have been as deep as that inspired by his piano pupil Giulietta Guicciardi. In fact another pianist, Dorothea von Ertmann, seems to be the most likely woman to be thought of by Beethoven as the ''Immortal Beloved''.

Therese von Brunsvik

Giulietta Guicciardi

Amalie von Sebald

The Last Symphony

Beethoven's last years were marked by illness and worry on the one hand, but by some monumental masterpieces on the other. He composed the *Missa Solemnis* between 1819 and 1823, and also the Ninth Symphony in about the same period. As with most of his work, Beethoven had made sketches of these compositions before he actually started writing them. He also wrote some more piano sonatas, the Diabelli Variations and the late string quartets. Then, towards the very end, there were sketches for a Tenth Symphony.

Despite the problems of his life, Beethoven had become a character in Vienna. The Viennese were fond, and even proud, of this eccentric man in their midst. But they were the last to realize that he was dying and in need of help. Beethoven was a proud man and did not suffer fools, or charity, easily, especially when it came from those closest to him.

In the fall of 1826 Beethoven went to stay with his surviving brother at Gneixendorf. He then returned to the Schwarzspanierhaus in Vienna, where he was to die. The *Missa Solemnis* and the Ninth Symphony, together with the late string quartets, were to be the last works from this great man.

Right: A sketch of Beethoven by Lyser. Although only in his fifties it is said that Beethoven looked and walked like a man in his seventies.

Below: The Missa Solemnis *was written for the Archduke Rudolf when he became Archbishop of Olmütz. He was Beethoven's former pupil and patron.*

Right: A portrait of Beethoven holding the Missa Solemnis *painted in 1818 or 1819. He did not complete the* Missa Solemnis *until 1823.*

Above: Beethoven's funeral procession. It is said that some 20,000 people packed the square outside the house.

Right: The study in the Schwarzspanierhaus in Vienna where Beethoven died on the 26th of March, 1827.

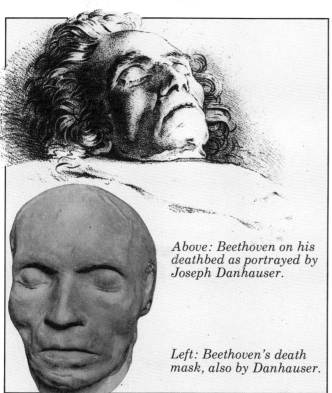

Above: Beethoven on his deathbed as portrayed by Joseph Danhauser.

Left: Beethoven's death mask, also by Danhauser.

Time Chart

Year	Beethoven's Life	Other Events
1770	Birth of Ludwig van Beethoven; Baptised on 17th December in the Church of St Remigius, Bonn.	Mozart in Italy; Birth of William Wordsworth and Georg Hegel; James Cook discovers Botany Bay, Australia.
1774	Beethoven's brother Caspar Anton Carl baptised on 8th April.	Louis XVI becomes King of France
1775	Beethoven's brother Nikolaus Johann baptised on 2nd October; The family move from the Rheingasse to the Neugasse.	American Revolution (until 1783); James Watt perfects his invention of the steam engine; Birth of Turner, Jane Austen and André Ampère; Jenner pioneers vaccination.
1776		Declaration of Independence; Adam Smith publishes *Wealth of Nations*; Birth of Constable.
1777	Palace fire at Bonn; The Beethoven family move back to the Rheingasse.	Bushnell invents the torpedo.
1778	Beethoven makes his musical debut in Bonn on 26th March.	War of Bavarian Succession (to 1779); La Scala in Milan opened; Death of Rousseau and Voltaire.
1779	Arrival in Bonn of Neefe. Beethoven receives viola and violin lessons from Rovantini.	James Cook murdered in Hawaii; Spain declares war on Britain (to 1783).
1781	Neefe becomes the Court organist; Death of Rovantini.	Herschel discovers the planet Uranus; Construction of the Siberian highway begun.
1782	Beethoven plays the organ at Court in Neefe's absence; Publishes the *Dressler Variations*, and is appointed continuo player in the court theater orchestra.	Birth of Paganini; Death of J C Bach.
1783	He dedicates three piano sonatas to the Elector Maximilian Friedrich; He composes Rondos in C and A.	First successful hot-air balloon; The Peace of Versailles ends American Revolution; Famine in Japan.
1784	Beethoven is appointed assistant court organist; He composes piano concerto in E flat.	Pitt's India Act (Government control of political affairs in India); Death of Dr Johnson.
1785	Beethoven composes three piano quartets.	Watt's invention of the two-cylinder engine and double-acting engine; Cartwright's mechanical loom.
1786	Birth of Beethoven's last sister Margaretha in May.	Birth of Weber; Death of Frederick II of Prussia.
1787	Beethoven visits Vienna to meet Mozart; Death of Beethoven's mother and youngest sister.	United States of America constitution signed; Death of Glück; Wilkinson's iron-hull ship built.
1788	Beethoven plays the viola in the court theater orchestra in Bonn.	First convicts transported from Britain to Australia; Birth of Byron.
1789	Beethoven composes two preludes for piano. Enrols at the University of Bonn.	Beginning of the French Revolution; George Washington made the first president of the United States.
1790	Meets Haydn in Bonn; Composes cantatas on the death of Emperor Joseph II and accession of Emperor Leopold II.	De Sivrac's *célérifère*, forerunner of the bicycle.
1791	Beethoven composes the *Ritterballet* and continues to play in the court orchestra.	Death of Mozart; The Bill of Rights (the first 10 amendments to the US constitution).
1792	Haydn returns to Bonn and Beethoven decides to go to Vienna with him for lessons; Death of Beethoven's father.	French revolutionary wars begin and France is declared a republic; Francis II becomes Holy Roman Emperor on the death of his father Leopold II; Birth of Rossini.
1794	Haydn returns to England and Beethoven goes to Albrechtsberger and Salieri for lessons; He publishes Op. 1 in Vienna and three piano trios.	First telegraph system established in France; US navy established.
1795	Beethoven's debut at the Burgtheater with Piano Concerto in B flat, Op.19; Composes Twelve Minuets and Twelve German Dances.	Third partition of Poland; Mungo Park explores the course of the Niger River.
1796	Visit to Prague, Dresden, Leipzig and Berlin; Composes string quartets, Op.4 and piano and wind quintet, Op.16 and cello sonatas, Op.5.	Napoleon Bonaparte leads French army and conquers most of Italy; Death of Empress Catherine II of Russia.
1797	Beethoven composes the Austrian battle song (*Kriegslied*), not a success; He finishes piano sonata, Op.7 and Rondo in C, Op.51, No 1.	Peace between Austria and France; Frederick William III becomes King of Prussia; Birth of Schubert and Donizetti.
1798	Beethoven returns to Prague; He publishes piano sonata, Op.10 and clarinet trio, Op.11; He works on *Pathétique* piano sonata, Op.13.	Horatio Nelson and the British fleet destroy the French fleet at Aboukir and end Napoleon's Egyptian campaign.
1799	Works on First Symphony, Op.21; Publishes *Pathétique*, three violin sonatas, Op.12 and two piano sonatas, Op.14.	Napoleon becomes the First Consul of France; Death of George Washington; Birth of Balzac.

Year	Beethoven's Life	Other Events
1800	Composes string quartets, Op.18, piano sonata Op.22, piano concerto No 3 and *Prometheus*.	French defeat the Austrians at the Battle of Marengo; Pius VII becomes Pope.
1801	Deafness becomes serious; Composes piano sonatas, Opp. 26–28. violin sonatas, Opp. 23 and 24 and string quintet, Op.29.	Death of Elector Maximilian Franz; Act of Union (1800) creates the United Kingdom; Birth of Bellini; Assassination of Paul I of Russia, Alexander I becomes Tsar; Robert Fulton produces the first submarine.
1802	Completes Second Symphony, Op.36; Writes the Heiligenstadt Testament; Composes piano sonatas, Op.31 and *Eroica* Variations for piano, Op.35.	Napoleon is made First Consul for life; Trevithick's track steam engine.
1803	Completes the oratorio *The Mount of Olives* and *Kreuzter* violin sonata, Op.47; Begins work on *Eroica* Op.55; Publication of violin (Op.30) and piano (Op.31) sonatas.	"Louisiana Purchase" by the US from France; War again between Britain and France; Birth of Berlioz; Robert Fulton perfects the steamboat.
1804	Completion of *Eroica* and piano sonatas, Opp.53 and 54; Begins work on *Leonore*, eventually to be known as *Fidelio*.	Napoleon crowns himself Emperor.
1805	First public performance of *Eroica* in April and of *Fidelio* in November; Completed piano sonata *Appassionata*, Op.57.	Napoleon in Vienna; British defeat Franco-Spanish fleet at the Battle of Trafalgar; French defeat Russians and Austrians at Austerlitz; Death of Schiller.
1806	Birth of nephew Karl.	Napoleon defeats Russians at Jena; Napoleon dissolves the Holy Roman Empire.
1807	Fourth Symphony, Op.60 and Mass in C, Op.86 completed.	Birth of Garibaldi.
1808	Completion of Fifth and Sixth Symphonies, Opp. 67 and 68, two piano trios, Op.70 and Choral Fantasia, Op.80.	Peninsular War in Spain (until 1814).
1809	Composes piano sonatas Opp. 78–81 and *Emperor* concerto.	French bombard Vienna; Death of Haydn; Birth of Mendelssohn, Darwin and Lincoln.
1810	Composes music to *Egmont*, Op.84 and string quartet, Op.95.	Simon Bolivar emerges as a major figure in South American politics; Birth of Schumann and Chopin.
1811	First visit to Teplitz; Completes piano trio, Op.97, *Archduke*; Works on the Seventh Symphony, *Ruins of Athens*, Op.113 and *King Stephan*, Op.117.	Paraguay gains independence from Spain; Birth of Liszt.
1812	Second visit to Teplitz where Beethoven meets Goethe; Completes Seventh and Eighth Symphonies.	Anglo-American War (until 1814); Napoleon retreats from Moscow; Birth of Charles Dickens.
1813	*Battle of Vittoria*, Op.91 given the first performance with the Seventh Symphony on 8th December.	Battle of Leipzig, Germans throw off Napoleon's domination; Battle of Vittoria, the French thrown out of Spain by Wellington; Birth of Verdi and Wagner.
1814	Revision of *Fidelio* and a performance in May. The work now a success; Completion of piano sonata, Op.90.	Napoleon exiled to Elba; Peace of Paris restores French borders of 1792; Congress of Vienna (to 1815); Louis XVIII becomes King of France.
1815	Death of brother Caspar Anton Carl; Composed piano and cello sonatas, Op.102.	Napoleon escapes from Elba and is defeated at the Battle of Waterloo; Prussia starts a German Confederation.
1816	Beethoven obtains legal custody of his nephew Karl, but later loses it; Completes piano sonata, Op.101 and *An die ferne Geliebte*, Op.98.	Davy invents the safety lamp; Birth of Charlotte Brontë; Argentina declares independence.
1818	Continues work on *Hammerklavier*; Oratorio commission from the Vienna *Gesellschaft*; Sketches for *Missa Solemnis*, Op.123.	British control dominates India; Chile becomes independent from Spain; Birth of Karl Marx.
1819	Completes *Hammerklavier* and works on *Missa Solemnis*.	Colombia gains independence.
1820	Lawsuit finally decided in Beethoven's favor; completes piano sonata, Op. 109, published the following year.	George IV becomes King of England; Revolutions in Spain and Portugal.
1821	Completes piano sonata, Op.110; First signs of liver disease.	Death of Napoleon; Greek war of independence against Turkey (succeeds in 1829); Peru becomes independent.
1822	Completes piano sonata, Op.111 and overture *The Consecration of the House*, Op.124; Meets Rossini.	Brazil is independent from Portugal; Birth of César Franck, Gregor Mendel and Louis Pasteur.
1823	*Missa Solemnis* completed, also Diabelli Variations, Op.120; Continues work on Ninth Symphony.	Spanish revolution crushed; Monroe Doctrine in the US; Liszt, aged 12, gives a concert in Vienna and meets Beethoven.
1825	Completion of string quartet, Op.132 and work on Op.130.	December revolt against the Tsar in Russia; Death of Salieri; Bolivia becomes independent.
1826	Beethoven composes quartets, Opp.131 and 135 and new finale for Op.130.	Russia and Persia at War (to 1828); Death of Weber.
1827	Beethoven dies on 26th March.	Death of William Blake; Wöhler discovers aluminum.

Beethoven's Greatest Works

Opera: *Fidelio*, Op. 72 (1804–05 in the original version known as *Leonore*). Revised in 1806 and 1814.

Mass: *Missa Solemnis*, Op. 123 (1819–23).

Choral music: Fantasia for piano, chorus and orchestra, Op.80 (1808).

Symphonies: No 1 in C, Op.21 (1799–1800); No 2 in D, Op.36 (1801–02); No 3 in E flat, Op.55 (1803), *Eroica*; No 4 in B flat, Op.60 (1806); No 5 in C minor, Op.67 (1804–08); No 6 in F, Op.68 (1807–08), *Pastoral*; No 7 in A, Op.92 (1811–12); No 8 in F, Op.93 (1812); and No 9 in D minor, Op.125 (1822–24), *Choral*.

Overtures: *Leonore* No 1, Op.138 (1805); *Leonore* No 2, Op.72a (1805); *Leonore* No 3, Op.72a (1806); *Coriolan*, Op.62 (1807); and also the overture from incidental music to *Egmont*, Op.84 (1810).

Concertos: Piano – No 1 in C, Op.15 (1798); No 2 in B flat, Op.19 (second version 1798–1801); No 3 in C minor, Op.37 (1800); No 4 in G, Op.58 (1805–06); No 5 in E flat, Op.73 (1809), *Emperor*; Violin – in D, Op.61 (1806); Piano, violin and cello – in C, Op.56 (1803–04).

String Quartets: Op.59 (1805–06), *Razumovsky*; E flat, Op.74 (1809), *Harp*; F minor, Op.95 (1810); E flat, Op.127 (1822–25); A minor, Op.132 (1825); B flat, Op.130 (1825, new finale 1826); B flat, Op.133 (1825), *Grosse fuge*, original finale of Op.130; C sharp minor, Op.131 (1826); and F, Op.135 (1826).

Piano solo: Sonatas in C minor, Op.13 (1798–99), *Pathétique*; C sharp minor, Op.27, No 2 (1801), *Moonlight*; C, Op.53 (1803–04), *Waldstein*; F minor, Op.57 (1804–05), *Appassionata*; E flat, Op.81a (1809–10), *Les Adieux*, and B flat, Op.106 (1817–19), *Hammerklavier*; Fifteen variations and a fugue in E flat, Op.35 (1802), on a theme from *The Creatures of Prometheus* (*Eroica* variations); Thirty-three variations in C, Op.120 (1823), on a waltz by Diabelli.

Glossary

Aria A vocal solo in an *opera, oratorio* or other musical work. It is usually in three parts.

Cantata A short piece of music for one or more soloists and an orchestra, and usually sung with a *chorus*.

Chamber music A type of music written for small groups of instruments. It was originally played in private rooms (chambers).

Chorus A group of people singing together, such as a church choir.

Concerto A piece of music in which a solo instrument, such as a violin, plays with an orchestra. A concerto usually has three movements.

Opera A play set to music for performance on the stage.

Oratorio A piece of music using soloists, *chorus* and orchestra. The subject has usually been taken from the Bible, such as Haydn's *Creation*.

Overture A piece of music which has been written as an introduction to an *opera* or other musical work.

Quartet A group of four musicians. A string quartet consists of two violinists, one cellist and one viola player.

Sonata A piece of instrumental music, usually with three or four movements.

Symphony A piece of music written for the orchestra, usually with three or four movements.

Trio A group of three musicians. A string trio consists of a violinist, a cellist and a viola player.

Index

Note: Page numbers in *italics* refer to illustrations.

Acknowledgements

Picture Research: Jackie Cookson
Photographs: With the authorization of the Beethoven-Haus, Bonn 12 *bottom right*, 13 *center*, 22, 23 *bottom left and right*, 25 *bottom*; Bildarchiv Preussicher Kulturbesitz 11 *center*, 19 *top left*, 23 *bottom center*; Dr Marietta Hausknost 2–3; Gesellschaft der Musikfreunde in Wien 25 *top left*; Graphische Sammlung Albertina 18–19 *bottom*; Hamlyn Group Picture Library 24 *bottom left*; Kunst-Dias Blauel/Theatermuseum München 20 *bottom*; Kunsthistorisches Museum, Vienna 4–5; Mansell Collection 7, 9, 12 *bottom left*, 14 *center*, 24 *top right*, 25 *center left*; Mary Evans Picture Library 24 *bottom right*; Osterreichische Nationalbibliothek 12 *center right*, 16, 19 *top right*, 20 *top right*, 25 *top right*; SNARK 17 *top right*; Stadtarchiv, Bonn/Hamlyn Group Picture Library 13 *top*; Stadtarchiv und Wissenschaftliche Stadtbibliothek, Bonn 14 *top and bottom*; ZEFA 10.

DATE DUE

APR 7 1983		
NOV 1 2 1985		
JAN 2 5 1991		
APR 3 0 1991		
MAR 1 8 1992		
APR 2 6 1993		
OCT 1 8 1993		
NOV 1 1 1993		
DEC 1 1993		
MAY 6 1994		
MAY 1 1995		
JAN 3 1 1997		
OCT 3 1 2007		
DEC - 2 2009		

HIGHSMITH 45-102   PRINTED IN U.S.A.

1610